THE CONCISE FIELD GUIDE TO AI 2ND EDITION

Because We Learned Some New Stuff

Mark Starcher

Scanmark LTD

SCANMARKLTD

INTRODUCTION

Okay, buckle up because the AI revolution is here, and it's weirding everyone out! But hold your horses, this ain't no snooze-fest textbook designed to melt your brain. Think of this as "AI for Dummies" but with way more sass and way less condescension. We're calling it the **Concise Field Guide to AI, 2nd Edition** because we have learned some new stuff since the 1st edition was released.

Let's be honest, AI is already calling the shots. It's the puppet master behind your Netflix recommendations, your social media feed, and maybe even that creepy Uber driver who never speaks. Ignoring it is like pretending the internet doesn't exist—good luck with that! This stuff is here to stay, and the sooner you get hip to it, the less likely you are to get trampled by the robot uprising (just kidding... mostly).

This book is your backstage pass to the wild world of generative AI, minus the boring lectures and pop quizzes. We're talking plain English, real-world examples, and maybe even a few spicy memes to keep things interesting.

Here's the lowdown on what you'll be getting into:

The Basics, But Not Like Your High School Teacher Taught Them: We'll break down all the fancy AI jargon—neural networks, deep learning, blah blah blah—in a way that even your goldfish could understand (okay, maybe not your goldfish).

The Cool Stuff That'll Make You Say "Whoa": Get ready to have your mind blown by the crazy things AI can do, from painting masterpieces and composing symphonies to diagnosing diseases and writing code (seriously, it's like magic, but with more math).

By the time you finish this book, you'll be able to:

Flex Your AI Knowledge Like a Boss:
Casually drop terms like "GANs" and
"transformers" at your next party and watch
everyone's eyes glaze over with admiration (or
confusion, but who cares?).

Decode the Matrix: You'll be able to see the
AI strings pulling the levers of the world around you, from targeted ads
to self-driving cars. Neo ain't got nothin' on you.

Unleash Your Inner AI Maestro: Who knows, maybe you'll be the
next AI art sensation or the creator of the next chart-topping AI-
generated hit. The possibilities are endless (and slightly terrifying).

So, grab your favorite beverage, put on your thinking cap (or a tinfoil hat, if
you're feeling paranoid), and get ready for a wild ride through the world of
generative AI.

To the AI that tried to write this book before me—
Thanks for all the drafts and none of the royalties.
This book and the accompanying graphics were produced, in part,
using various AI tools mentioned in this book.

CONTENTS

1

CHAPTER 1: WHAT IS AI, REALLY?

◆ ◆ ◆

L et's dive into AI—the thing everyone's buzzing about. Robots are taking over, computers are going all sentient, and the works. But hold up! Before we start digging bunkers, let's clear some things up. AI is cool, but it's not your sci-fi nightmare (probably).

AI: Not Just for Hollywood

In simple terms, AI means making machines smart—not just "solve-a-Rubik's-Cube" smart, but smart enough to mimic human intelligence. Think about what you do daily: recognize faces, understand language, and make decisions. AI aims to make computers do the same, sometimes even better. But don't expect C-3PO just yet. AI ranges from basic calculators to systems that write poetry or compose music.

A Blast from the Past: AI's Roots

AI isn't the new kid on the block. It dates back to the mid-20th century, with geniuses like Alan Turing, who proposed the "Turing Test"—AI's first reality show.

Think of AI as teaching your computer to be human. It's been a rollercoaster of hype and disappointment, but each cycle brought discoveries, leading to today's AI boom.

Key Milestones in AI History

1950s: Birth of AI
- ◆ Alan Turing proposes the Turing Test.
- ◆ "Artificial Intelligence" is coined at the Dartmouth Conference.

1960s-70s: Early Explorations
- ◆ Development of programs like ELIZA, a chatbot.
- ◆ Introduction of Expert Systems.

1980s: The First AI Winter
- ◆ Hype exceeds reality; progress slows.

1990s: AI Renaissance
- ◆ IBM's Deep Blue beats chess champion Garry Kasparov.

2000s: Machine Learning Takes Off
- ◆ Breakthroughs in Deep Learning.

2010s: Deep Learning Boom
- ◆ AlexNet wins the ImageNet competition.
- ◆ Google's AlphaGo beats Go champion Lee Sedol.

2020s: AI Everywhere
- ◆ From voice assistants to self-driving cars.

Busting AI Myths Like a Boss

Let's crush some juicy AI myths:

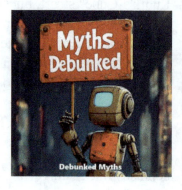

Myth #1: AI is about robots. Nope, AI is the brains, not the metal overlords. It's on your phone, laptop, or maybe your toaster (someday).

Myth #2: AI will steal all our jobs. It might automate some tasks, but it also creates new opportunities. Think job reshuffle, not apocalypse.

Myth #3: AI will become sentient and take over. Deep breaths. AI isn't plotting world dominance. It's a powerful tool, but still just a tool.

AI in Your Pocket: Everyday Examples

You probably interact with AI daily without realizing it.

Netflix Recommendations: Creepy-good at suggesting shows you'll like.
Spam Filters: Saving you from questionable emails.
Voice Assistants: Siri, Alexa, and Google Assistant—ready to answer questions and tell terrible jokes.

AI is already woven into our lives, making things more accessible, efficient, and sometimes creepy. Instead of fearing it, let's embrace the possibilities.

Defining AI: Beyond the Hype

AI aims to create machines capable of tasks that require human intelligence, like:

Learning: Acquiring knowledge through experience.
Reasoning: Solving problems and making decisions.
Perception: Interpreting sensory inputs.
Language Understanding: Processing human language.

AI, Machine Learning, and Deep Learning: Untangling the Web

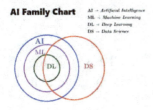

Picture AI as the biggest Russian doll. Inside it is ML, teaching computers to learn from data. Nestled within ML is DL, using neural networks inspired by the human brain. These concepts intersect with data science, which uses statistical tools to make sense of information.

Artificial Intelligence (AI)

AI is the big umbrella term for machines that perform tasks that require human-like intelligence. It's like teaching a toaster to write a symphony or a blender to solve a Rubik's cube.

AI categories:

Narrow AI: Excellent at one task, like Siri telling you the weather.

General AI: The dream machine that can do any intellectual task.

3

Super AI: Sci-fi stuff—machines smarter than humans.

AI is used in various applications, from self-driving cars to virtual assistants. But remember, AI is only as good as the data and algorithms we feed it.

Machine Learning (ML)

ML is like teaching a baby to walk, except it's a computer. You feed it data, and it finds patterns to make predictions or decisions without explicit programming.

Types of ML:

Supervised Learning: Like a strict teacher with labeled examples.

Unsupervised Learning: Letting a kid loose in a candy store to find patterns.

Reinforcement Learning: The machine learns by trial and error

ML is used in recommending products, detecting fraud, and more. But beware—biased data leads to flawed decisions.

Deep Learning (DL)

DL is the overachiever, creating complex neural networks that mimic the human brain. These networks learn from data to become really good at tasks like recognizing cat pictures or generating fake faces.

DL can do:

Image and Speech Recognition: Identifying objects and understanding speech.

Natural Language Processing: Analyzing and generating human language.

Autonomous Vehicles: Powering self-driving cars.

Beating Humans at Games: Mastering games like Go and chess.

Data Science (DS)

Data Science is like being a detective, but you're solving data mysteries instead of solving crimes. It involves collecting, cleaning, analyzing, and interpreting data to make predictions.

The process includes:

Data Collection: Gathering data from various sources.

Data Cleaning: Wrangling data into shape.

Exploratory Data Analysis: Getting to know your data.

Machine Learning: Teaching a computer to make predictions.

Interpretation and Communication: Making sense of findings.

AI: More Than Just Robots Gone Rogue

AI is about teaching computers to think—or at least mimic thinking—without human guidance.

Forget Analysis, Let's Talk Creation

Generative AI is where things get wild. It's not just crunching numbers; it's creating. Think poems, paintings, music, even code—all by AI.

The AI Art Show: Text, Images, Audio, Video, and Code

Generative AI isn't just a one-trick pony:

- **Text**: AI-written stories and news articles.
- **Images**: AI-generated visuals—from photorealistic to abstract.
- **Audio**: Composing music and sound effects.
- **Video**: AI-generated animations and effects.
- **Code**: AI writing code for websites and apps.

From Poems to Pills: AI is Changing the World

Generative AI is reshaping industries:

- **Creative Arts**: Partnering with artists for new creations.
- **Healthcare**: Designing drugs and analyzing medical images.
- **Marketing and Advertising**: Creating personalized campaigns.
- **Education**: Personalizing learning experiences.
- **Research and Development**: Speeding up scientific discovery.

The Generative Revolution is just starting. AI is now a creative collaborator, blurring the lines between human and artificial imagination. Buckle up, because the future is a wild ride!

Next we do a deep dive into the computer magic behind generative AI.

CHAPTER 2: INSIDE THE BLACK BOX: HOW AI ACTUALLY WORKS (SPOILER ALERT: IT'S MATH)

◆ ◆ ◆

Okay, so AI can write poems, paint pictures, and maybe even swipe your job (just kidding... mostly). But how does it work? What's inside that mysterious AI brain? It's time to crack open the black box, but don't worry, you won't need a PhD in computer science to get this.

Machine Learning: AI's Crash Course in Being Smart (Sort Of)

Teaching Baby

Imagine teaching a baby to recognize a cat. You show them fluffy felines, chanting "cat" like a maniac. Eventually, their brain connects the dots. Machine learning is like that but with computers instead of babies (and fewer diaper changes).

We feed AI tons of data—text, images, music, you name it—and tell it what it is. The AI then gorges on this data buffet, finding patterns we humans might miss. It's like AI playing a giant game of "Where's Waldo," except it's looking for the secret sauce of intelligence.

From Data to Genius (or at Least Competence): The AI Learning Journey

AI thrives on data. The more data, the better it learns. ChatGPT 3.5 was trained on 300 billion words, while Gemini Pro 1.5 is estimated to have a training dataset of 5.5 trillion tokens. So, the next time you're amazed by AI, remember it's all thanks to neural networks, crunching data, and learning patterns one digital synapse at a time. Maybe one day, AI can even explain *how* it does it. Until then, we'll just enjoy the show.

Neural Networks: AI's Brainpower (Not Literally)

So, how does AI learn? Enter neural networks, the rockstars of AI. Inspired by the human brain (but less squishy), they're made of interconnected nodes, like a digital spiderweb. Each node processes info and passes it on like a game of digital hot potato. As AI learns, node connections strengthen or weaken, fine-tuning its pattern recognition and prediction skills. It's like AI building its mental map of the world, one data point at a time.

GANs, Transformers, and Other AI Superstars (Because Every Field Needs Its Celebrities)

Just like there are different types of human brains (some good at math, others at interpretive dance), there are different neural networks, each with its own superpowers:

- **GANs (Generative Adversarial Networks):** The rebels of AI, constantly trying to outsmart each other. Imagine two AIs, one creating content, the other judging it. They battle until the creator makes stuff so good it fools even the harshest critic. That's how we get those hyperrealistic AI-generated images and videos.
- **Convolutional Neural Networks (CNNs):** The image masters. They dissect images into tiny pieces, looking for patterns like edges and shapes. They're like digital art critics but give you accurate image recognition instead of pretentious pronouncements.

- **Recurrent Neural Networks (RNNs):** The memory keepers. They remember past inputs to predict the future, like a psychic octopus (but less slimy). They can generate text and music, but they're also prone to going off the rails, like a toddler on a sugar rush.
- **Transformers:** The language whizzes. They understand and generate text with mind-blowing accuracy. They're the brains behind chatbots, translators, and AI-written poems that probably make Shakespeare roll in his grave (with envy).
- **State Space Models**: State space models (SSMs) are a class of probabilistic graphical models that represent a system as a sequence of hidden states evolving over time, where each state influences the observed data.

The Art of Neural Forgery: GANs and the Great Creative Disruption

If the artificial intelligence world were a London private members' club, Generative Adversarial Networks (GANs) would be the provocateurs causing a delightful ruckus in the smoking room. Imagine, if you will, a highly sophisticated game of cat and mouse, where both participants happen to be neural networks with rather expensive tastes.

Conceived by Ian Goodfellow in 2014 (reportedly during a pub debate, though our fact-checkers remain skeptical), GANs operate on a principle that would make any hedge fund manager proud: perpetual competition. The architecture consists of two networks – a "generator" that creates fake data and a "discriminator" that attempts to spot the forgeries. Think of it as an endless sparring match between a masterful counterfeiter and an increasingly exasperated art authenticator.

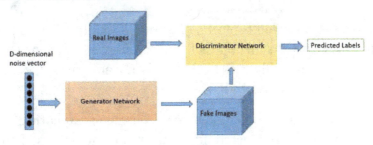

The generator starts off producing what might charitably be called "abstract art" – the sort that makes even Picasso look conventional. Through iterative training, it gradually improves its craft, while the discriminator becomes increasingly sophisticated in its detection methods. It's rather like watching a high-stakes game of poker where both players are learning the rules mid-game.

The results have been nothing short of remarkable. GANs now create everything from fake faces that look more real than your LinkedIn profile picture to artificial luxury goods that would make Bond Street boutiques nervous. They've even ventured into the realm of creating synthetic financial data, though we're assured this has nothing to do with recent market volatility.

Perhaps most impressively, GANs have managed to democratize creativity itself, though not without raising thorny questions about authenticity and ownership that would keep a City law firm billing for decades. They represent the perfect marriage of creativity and competition – a combination that, coincidentally, describes most successful financial innovations.

Convolutional Neural Networks (CNNs): Seeing the World in Pixels

Want a computer to recognize a dog in a picture? That's where CNNs come in. They break down images into smaller pieces, applying "convolution" to find patterns like edges and shapes. They're like digital detectives, piecing together clues to understand the whole picture.

Beyond the Buzzwords: CNNs Explained Over an Imaginary Martini

In the increasingly crowded pantheon of artificial intelligence, convolutional neural networks (CNNs) stand out as the overachievers of the machine learning family – think of them as the hedge fund managers of the algorithmic world, but with better social skills.

Born from an ambitious attempt to mimic the human visual cortex, CNNs have become the go-to architecture for image recognition tasks, displaying an almost uncanny ability to distinguish between pictures of cats and dogs – a feat that, while seemingly trivial, had proved remarkably challenging for traditional computing approaches.

The "convolutional" part of their name comes from the mathematical operation they employ, though one suspects the terminology was chosen primarily to make computer scientists sound clever at dinner parties. In essence, these networks scan images through a series of filters – imagine a fussy butler inspecting a mansion room by room, but at lightning speed.

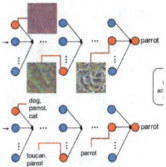

What sets CNNs apart is their hierarchical learning approach. The initial layers detect basic features like edges and colours (rather like a junior analyst spotting obvious market trends), while deeper layers combine these insights to recognize increasingly complex patterns (more akin to a seasoned fund manager spotting subtle market inefficiencies).

The real genius lies in their ability to maintain spatial relationships while reducing computational complexity – a bit like knowing which parts of the FT are worth reading and which can be skimmed over during your morning commute.

These networks have proved so successful that they've expanded well beyond image recognition into video analysis, natural language processing, and even drug discovery. They've become the Swiss Army knife of deep learning, though like any good tool, they're only as clever as the humans wielding them.

For all their sophistication, CNNs remain surprisingly susceptible to being fooled by adversarial examples – rather like how a bespoke-suited analyst might occasionally mistake a bear market for a mere correction.

Recurrent Neural Networks (RNNs): The Time Travelers of AI

RNNs remember past inputs, making them great for sequential data like text and speech. They're like AI fortune tellers, trying to predict the next word or note. But they can be unpredictable, prone to generating gibberish as easily as poetry. Training them is like herding cats – good luck with that.

Memory Merchants: RNNs and the Art of Neural Sequence Surfing

If convolutional neural networks are the hedge fund managers of machine learning, recurrent neural networks (RNNs) are the City traders with a peculiar obsession for connecting dots through time – imagine a quantum physicist meets a day trader with a dash of short-term memory thrown in for good measure.

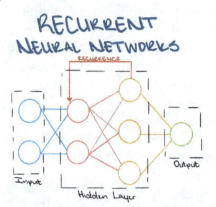

Unlike their more straightforward cousins, RNNs possess what one might call an algorithmic memory, allowing them to maintain context across sequential data. Think of them as that colleague who somehow remembers every detail from last quarter's earnings calls but occasionally forgets where they left their phone.

The "recurrent" aspect refers to their habit of feeding previous outputs back into the system – rather like a regulatory feedback loop, but considerably more helpful. This architectural quirk enables them to process data sequences, making them particularly adept at tasks involving time series, text, or any data where context is king.

However, these networks faced an early identity crisis (and functionality) with the infamous "vanishing gradient problem" – a mathematical affliction that made them lose track of long-term dependencies, much like a trader who can't quite remember why they bought those penny stocks last month.

The breakthrough came with the introduction of Long Short-Term Memory (LSTM) networks and their slightly more streamlined siblings, GRUs. These sophisticated variants added internal memory cells, acting rather like a neural notepad that could selectively remember or forget information – think of it as a Bloomberg terminal with an excellent personal assistant.

RNNs have since become the backbone of everything from machine translation to stock price prediction, though their success in the latter might be charitably described as "mixed". They excel at tasks requiring sequential understanding, from predicting the next word in a sentence to forecasting weather patterns – though, much like weather forecasters, they're not always right.

Transformers: The Masters of Language

Transformers are the language gurus of AI. They use "self-attention" to focus on the most critical parts of a sentence, like reading a gossip magazine and zeroing in on the juicy bits. They excel at translation, summarization, chatbots, and text generation. They're still evolving, but they're already transforming how we interact with language.

The Attention Economy: How Transformers Became AI's Blue-Chip Stock

In the ever-evolving circus of artificial intelligence, Transformer networks have achieved what every City analyst dreams of: turning complexity into cold, hard market dominance. Born in Google's labs in 2017, they've become the architectural equivalent of a FTSE 100 stalwart, but with somewhat better growth prospects.

At their core, Transformers solved the sequence processing problem with all the elegance of a perfectly executed merger: instead of painfully processing data step by step like their RNN predecessors, they deployed the now-famous "attention mechanism"—imagine a highly efficient personal assistant who can instantly spot relevant connections in a sea of information without requiring a corner office.

The architecture's clever parallel processing approach means it can handle relationships between parts of its input simultaneously, like a trader monitoring multiple markets without the traditional requirement for eight computer screens. This self-attention mechanism has proved so effective that previous sequential processing methods look about as efficient as ticker tape.

Their scalability has led to an arms race of ever-larger models, with parameters counted in the billions – numbers that would make even a quantitative fund manager blush. GPT, BERT, and their increasingly

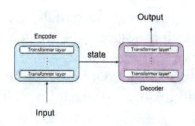

well-heeled descendants have demonstrated an almost unsettling ability to understand and generate human-like text, though occasionally with the accuracy of a slightly overconfident junior analyst.

Perhaps most remarkably, Transformers have achieved that rarest of feats in technology: becoming genuinely indispensable. Their influence extends from language processing to protein folding, making them the closest thing AI has to a universal architecture – though, like any universal solution, they come with universal energy bills to match.

The Quest for Post-Transformer Supremacy: A 2025 Field Report

While Transformers remain the reigning champions of AI's premier league, several upstart architectures are making waves in the paddock – though none has yet managed to unseat the incumbent fully.

State Space Models (SSMs) and **Mamba** architectures have emerged as intriguing challengers. Promising similar performance with significantly reduced computational overhead, they're the equivalent of a lean fintech startup eyeing the

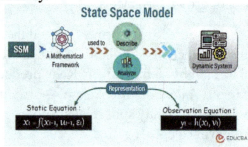

bloated infrastructure of traditional banks. Early 2024 benchmarks suggest they can process sequences up to 5x faster than traditional Transformers, though they still find their footing in absolute performance.

RetNet (Retention Networks) is another fascinating contender. It offers the attention mechanism's benefits without its quadratic computational costs. Rather like a highly efficient back-office automation system, it claims to deliver similar results with substantially reduced resource requirements.

Perhaps most intriguingly, hybrid architectures combining Transformer-like attention with alternative approaches are gaining traction. These "best of both worlds" models suggest the future may lie not in wholesale replacement but in clever architectural arbitrage.

However, like the perpetually predicted death of equities, proclamations of the Transformer's demise appear premature. Tech giants' massive investments in Transformer infrastructure—think of it as the AI equivalent of Bloomberg terminal lock-in—mean any successor faces significant adoption hurdles.

We're in a period of architectural exploration rather than revolution. The post-Transformer era may be coming, but like any good market transition, it's likely to be more evolution than disruption.

Next, we look at prompting -- a way to communicate intelligently with AI models.

16

CHAPTER 3: PROMPTING: SPEAKING THE AI LANGUAGE

◆ ◆ ◆

A I prompting is the art and science of communicating effectively with artificial intelligence, specifically generative models, to guide them toward producing desired outputs. It's like giving clear and specific instructions to a highly skilled but literal-minded artist or writer.

Here's a breakdown of the critical aspects:

1. Understanding the Model:

Different AI models have different strengths and weaknesses.

- Text-based models like Gemini or ChatGPT 4o generate human-like text, while others like DALL-E 3 specialize in creating images from textual descriptions.
- Knowing your model's capabilities is crucial for crafting effective prompts.

2. Elements of a Prompt:

A well-crafted prompt typically includes:

- **Instruction**: This tells the AI what you want it to do. Be clear and specific.
- **Context**: Provide background information or examples to guide the AI's understanding.
- **Constraints**: Specify any limitations or requirements for the output (e.g., length, style, format).

3. Prompt Engineering Techniques:

- **Keywording**: Use relevant keywords to steer the AI towards the desired topic.

- **Example Providing**: Show the AI what you want by providing examples.

- **Style and Tone Specification**: Use descriptive words to indicate the desired style (e.g., formal, humorous, poetic) and tone (e.g., positive, negative, informative).

- **Persona Adoption**: Ask the AI to respond as a specific persona (e.g., "Write a poem from the perspective of a cat.")

- **Iterative Refinement**: Don't be afraid to experiment and refine your prompts based on the AI's output.

Beyond the Basics:

- **Negative Prompting**: While we often focus on what we want the AI to generate, specifying what we don't wish to can be equally important. This is called negative prompting. For example, in image generation, you might add "no blurry backgrounds" or "no human faces" to refine the output.

- **Prompt Chaining** involves using the output of one prompt as the input for another, creating a chain of AI-generated content. For example, you could first ask the AI to generate a story outline and then use that outline as a prompt to develop the full story.

- **Parameter Tweaking**: Many AI models have adjustable parameters that influence the output.

    Temperature controls the randomness (higher temperature = more creative and unpredictable results).

    Top_k limits the AI's word choices to the most likely candidates (lower top_k = more focused and coherent output).

- **Fine-tuning** involves training an AI model on a specific dataset to improve performance on a particular task. For example, you could fine-tune a text generation model on a dataset of Shakespearean sonnets to generate text in a similar style.

Emerging Trends:

- **Multimodal Prompting**: This involves using multiple input modalities, such as text and images, to guide AI generation. For example, you could provide an image and a caption as a prompt for a story or a poem.
- **Prompt Engineering as Code**: Researchers are developing programming languages designed explicitly for crafting and managing complex AI prompts. This will enable more sophisticated and automated prompting workflows.

Prompt Examples:

Text Generation:

Prompt 1:

Instruction: Write a short story about a time traveler who meets their younger self.

Context: The time traveler is from a dystopian future and is trying to prevent it.

Constraints: Keep it under 500 words and focus on the emotional impact of the encounter.

This prompt provides clear instructions, context for the story, and constraints to guide the AI.

Prompt 2:

Instruction: Tweet about the importance of conservation.

Style and Tone: Use a persuasive and urgent tone, appealing to people's emotions.

Constraints: Keep it under 280 characters and include relevant hashtags.

This prompt specifies a tweet's desired style, tone, and platform-specific constraints.

Image Generation:

Prompt 1:

> **Instruction**: Generate an image of a futuristic cityscape.
>
> **Context**: Imagine a city with towering skyscrapers, flying cars, and neon lights.
>
> **Style**: Use a cyberpunk aesthetic with dark colors and a gritty atmosphere.

This prompt clearly defines the desired image, including context and style.

Prompt 2:

> **Instruction**: Create an image of a cat wearing a tiny hat.
>
> **Example**: [Provide a reference image of a cat wearing a hat]
>
> **Constraints**: Make the cat look surprised and the hat slightly too big.

This prompt uses an example image and specific constraints to guide the AI's creative output.

Ethical Considerations:

Bias Amplification: AI models are trained on massive datasets, which can contain biases present in the real world. Awareness of these biases and using prompting techniques to mitigate their impact is important.

Misinformation and Manipulation: AI-generated content can be incredibly realistic, making using these technologies responsibly and ethically crucial.

The Future of Prompting:

As AI models become more sophisticated, prompting will become an even more powerful and versatile tool for creativity, communication, and problem-solving. In the coming years, we can expect to see new prompting techniques, tools, and applications emerge.

Pushing the Boundaries:

- **Interactive Storytelling**: Imagine using AI prompting to co-create dynamic stories that evolve based on user choices. You provide the initial prompt, and the AI generates narrative branches, characters, and dialogue, creating a truly interactive experience.

- **Personalized Learning**: AI prompting can revolutionize education by generating customized learning materials tailored to individual student needs and learning styles.
- **AI-Assisted Design**: From website layouts to product prototypes, AI prompting can assist designers by generating creative concepts and variations based on specific requirements and constraints.

The Big Picture:

AI prompting is more than just a technique; it's a fundamental shift in how we interact with computers. It allows us to communicate with AI more naturally and intuitively, bridging the gap between human creativity and artificial intelligence. As AI technology advances, prompting will play an increasingly important role in shaping the future of various industries and aspects of our lives.

Conclusion:

Effective AI prompting is an iterative process that involves understanding the model, crafting clear instructions, and experimenting with different techniques. Mastering the art of prompting can unlock AI's full potential and generate impressive and creative outputs.

Next, we delve into the world of generative text in Chapter 4.

22

CHAPTER 4: WORDS COME ALIVE: TEXT GENERATION

◆ ◆ ◆

Welcome, dear reader, to the magical world of text generation! AI isn't just about crunching numbers or identifying cats in photos. No, it's about creating stories, poems, articles, and even code. It's like having Shakespeare, Hemingway, and Ada Lovelace rolled into one digital entity. How cool is that?

How AI Writes Stories, Poetry, Articles, and Even Code

Imagine if your laptop suddenly decided it wanted to be the next J.K. Rowling. Or if your phone starts spouting poetry like Robert Frost. That's pretty much what AI text generation is all about. AI can craft prose, verse, and even functional software using complex algorithms and vast datasets.

Take stories, for instance. AI models like GPT (**Generative Pre-trained Transformer**) can generate entire novels based on prompts. You give it a setting, characters, and a basic plot, and it'll whip up a narrative that might just make you forget it's not human.

When it comes to poems, AI can mimic styles from haikus to sonnets. It can even generate free verse that reads like it came from the mind of a tortured artist. Just don't expect it to have a deep, existential crisis. Yet.

◆ ◆ ◆

AI text generation is like a box of chocolates—you never know what you're going to get

❖ ❖ ❖

It can generate informative articles on almost any topic. From Roman Empire history to the latest trends in vegan cuisine, AI has you covered. And if you need some code? Well, AI can help with that, too. Tools like Codex can generate functional snippets in multiple programming languages, making it a coder's best friend.

Examples of Text-Based Generative AI Tools

Let's talk about some of the rock stars of he AI text generation world.

First up, **ChatGPT**. This tool is like the Swiss Army knife of text generation. Need a story? It's got you.

ChatGPT-4o

Need advice on how to bake a cake? Done. Want to know what the meaning of life is? Well, it'll give you a pretty good guess. ChatGPT can converse, offer suggestions, and generate text on almost any topic.

Then there's **Claude**. The Claude family of language models is a series of large language models developed by **Anthropic.** These feed on vast amounts of text data from the internet, allowing them to engage in a wide range of natural language tasks such as question-answering, text generation, and language understanding.

Google developed **Gemini 1.5,** an AI language model. It is an improved version of the original Gemini model, with language understanding and enhancements in generation capabilities. Gemini 1.5 is designed to engage in more natural and

Gemini 1.5

coherent conversations and to provide more accurate and relevant responses to a wide range of queries. The model has been trained on a vast corpus of data, allowing it to draw upon a deep knowledge base to assist users with tasks such as question answering, task completion, and open-ended dialogue.

Meta's artificial intelligence research division (formerly Facebook) created **Llama,** a sizable language model. It is a powerful and versatile AI system that can be used for various natural language process

  ing tasks, such as text generation, question answering, and language understanding. Llama is based on the Transformer architecture, which has become the dominant approach in large language models. The model has been trained on massive amounts of textual data, allowing it to understand language and generate human-like text on various topics deeply.

Grok is an AI chatbot developed by xAI, designed to answer questions humorously and offer access to real-time information through its connection to the internet.

Exploring the Ethical Considerations of AI-Generated Content

But wait. It's not all sunshine and rainbows in the land of AI-generated text. We must address serious ethical issues.

Plagiarism

We need to discuss the world of transformer-based language models and their little plagiarism problem. It's going to get really ugly, really fast.

These so-called "state-of-the-art" AI models, like Llama, ChatGPT, and Gemini 1.5, are glorified copy-paste machines. They scour the internet, hoovering up every bit of text they can get their digital mitts on, and then they spit it back out, pretending it's their original work. It's like many high school students trying to pass off Wikipedia articles as homework assignments.

The problem is that these models don't just regurgitate verbatim quotes; they learn the patterns and connections in the data, allowing them to generate scarily similar text to the original. So, you end up with AI-generated content, a seamless mashup of stolen material wrapped up in a neat bow of fluency and coherence. It's a literary tur

ducken, but instead of a chicken inside a duck inside a turkey, it's a bunch of plagiarized material inside re plagiarized material. And the kicker is that it's

not just academic writing or content generation at risk. These models are being used for all sorts of high-stakes applications, from legal documents to medical research. Can you imagine an

AI lawyer plagiarizing through a court case or a doctor's report that's just a jumble of copied medical text? It's a recipe for disaster, folks.

◆ ◆ ◆

These so-called "state-of-the-art" AI models, like Llama, ChatGPT, and Gemini 1.5, are glorified copy-paste machines

◆ ◆ ◆

So, while the AI research community is trying to figure out how to fix this mess, the rest of us wonder, "Hey, did Skynet just steal my term paper?" It's a brave new world filled with many unoriginal ideas.

Bias

Another elephant in the room regarding these so-called "cutting-edge" transformer models is the bias problem. It's like these AI systems are a bunch of drunk uncles at a family reunion, spouting off their half-baked opinions and passing them off as facts.

Take ChatGPT and Gemini 1.5, for example. These models are trained on mountains of online data, right? Well, guess what that data is full of? Yep, you guessed it—a helping of human biases, prejudices, and nonsense. It's like feeding a kid a steady diet of tabloid magazines and expecting them to have a nuanced understanding of the world.

And it's not just your run-of-the-mill biases. These models can pick up on all sorts of unsavory stuff, from racist and sexist language to conspiracy theories and outright falsehoods. It's like having a robot assistant who's been brainwashed by your aunt, who thinks the moon landing was faked.

◆ ◆ ◆

These models are so complex, and the training data is so vast that it's like trying to find a needle in a haystack.

◆ ◆ ◆

These biases don't just lurk in the background, oh no. They come out to play in the model's outputs, like a bad stand-up comedian at an open mic night. You could ask Llama a seemingly innocent question, and the next thing you know, it's spouting off some half-baked opinion about politics or gender that's straight out of the 1950s.

And let's not forget the cherry on top of this biased sundae—the fact that it's nearly impossible to eliminate these issues. These models are so complex, and the training data is so vast that it's like finding a needle in a haystack. It's enough to make you want to throw your hands up and return to using a good old-fashioned Magic 8-Ball for all your decision-making needs.

Authenticity and Attribution

Let's start with the whole attribution problem, shall we? These transformer models are magpies, swooping down and snatching up bits of text from all over the internet. And then they just slap it all together, hoping no one will notice that it's a Frankenstein's monster of plagiarized material. They're trying to pass off a collage of celebrity magazine clippings as their autobiography.

The worst part is that these models are so darn good at imitating human language that it's nearly impossible to tell when they're just regurgitating someone else's work. It's like having a con artist in your midst, spinning a web of lies and half-truths, and you're just sitting there, scratching your head, wondering if anything they're saying is even remotely authentic.

These transformer models aren't just struggling with attribution, oh no. They have a whole identity crisis going on. They're trained on all this data and can use it to generate all sorts of content, from poetry to code. But at the end of the day, are they the ones creating this stuff, or are they just a glorified copy-and-paste machine masquerading as a creative genius?

It's enough to make you question the very nature of AI and whether these models are brilliant or just good at mimicry. It's like having a parrot that can recite Shakespeare, but you're never quite sure if it understands what it's saying.

So, there you have it, folks—the identity crisis of the transformer models. It's a wild ride of plagiarism, impersonation, and many unanswered questions. Maybe we should just stick to good old-fashioned human authors, where at least we know the work is genuinely theirs (or at least, we hope it is).

◆ ◆ ◆

These transformer models are magpies, swooping down and snatching up bits of text from all over the internet.

◆ ◆ ◆

More Examples of Text-Based Generative AI Tools

General Purpose Writing & Content Creation:

Jasper.ai: A popular choice for marketing copy, blog posts, social media content, and more. It offers various templates and a user-friendly interface. It is known for its relatively high output quality and ease of use.

Copy.ai: Similar to Jasper, Copy.ai focuses on generating marketing copy quickly. It excels at short-form content like ad copy, social media captions, and product descriptions. It's known for its speed and affordability.

Rytr: A budget-friendly option that still delivers decent quality text generation for various purposes, including blog posts, articles, and social media content. It's a good starting point for users exploring AI writing tools.

Writesonic: Another versatile tool that covers a wide range of writing needs, from blog posts and articles to product descriptions and ad copy. It offers different writing styles and tones.

Scalenut: Positions itself as an SEO-focused content creation platform. It helps with keyword research, content planning, and AI writing, aiming to create content that ranks well in search engines.

Specialized AI Writing Tools:

ShortlyAI: Designed for long-form content creation, such as blog posts, articles, and stories. It emphasizes a minimalist interface to minimize distractions and encourage creative flow. Recently acquired by Jasper.

Sudowrite: Caters to creative writers, offering features like story idea generation, character development assistance, and stylistic suggestions. It's designed to help writers overcome writer's block and enhance their storytelling.

Article Forge: This tool generates entire articles on a given topic. It aims to automatically create unique, SEO-friendly content, though the quality can vary.

NotebookLM is an AI-powered note-taking and research assistant that helps users understand and interact with complex information. By uploading documents, users can create a personalized AI assistant that can answer questions, generate summaries, and even create audio

NotebookLM

Think Smarter, Not Harder

Try NotebookLM

overviews of the content. This tool aims to streamline the research process and provide deeper insights from various sources.

Code Generation:

GitHub Copilot: Developed by GitHub and OpenAI, Copilot assists developers by suggesting code completions and generating entire functions in real-time. It supports various programming languages and integrates directly into popular code editors.

Tabnine: Another AI-powered code completion tool that works with various IDEs and programming languages. It learns from your coding style and provides personalized suggestions to improve coding efficiency.

Now that you've seen how AI creates textual material, we delve into the world of AI image generation in Chapter 5.

CHAPTER 5: PAINTING WITH PIXELS: IMAGE GENERATION

◆ ◆ ◆

W elcome to the wild and wacky world of AI image generation, where pixels get a personality, and your computer suddenly becomes Picasso. We're diving into how AI creates realistic and fantastical images, the most remarkable tools out there, and the potential of AI in art and design. So grab your digital paintbrush, and let's get pixelated.

How AI Creates Realistic and Fantastical Images

The Magic Behind the Pixels

Creating images with AI isn't just about slapping some code together and hoping for the best. No, no. It's a bit like teaching a robot to dream. Here's how it goes down:

Training Time: AI models, like Generative Adversarial Networks (GANs), are trained on massive datasets of images, including anything from photos of cats to classical paintings.

Generator and Discriminator: Think of GANs as a dynamic duo. The generator creates images from scratch while the discriminator evaluates them. The generator wants to deceive the discriminator into thinking the images are real, and the discriminator seeks to catch the generator out. This game of cat-and-mouse continues until the generated images look legit.

31

Creativity Unleashed: Once trained, the AI can generate surprisingly realistic or deliciously surreal images. Want a cat with butterfly wings? Done. How about a hyper-realistic portrait of a fictional character? Easy peasy.

The Technical Wizardry

To truly appreciate the magic, let's break down the core technologies behind AI image generation:

Generative Adversarial Networks (GANs): Introduced by Ian Goodfellow and his team in 2014, GANs have revolutionized image generation. They consist of two neural networks—the generator and the discriminator—locked in a perpetual game of one-upmanship. The generator tries to create convincing images while the discriminator evaluates them for authenticity. Over time, both networks improve, resulting in highly realistic images.

Variational Autoencoders (VAEs): VAEs are another type of neural network that generates images. Unlike GANs, VAEs encode input data into a latent space and then decode it back into an image. This process allows for smooth interpolation between images, making VAEs great for generating variations and exploring creative possibilities.

Diffusion Models: These models, like Stable Diffusion, generate images by gradually transforming random noise into coherent images. They work by reversing a process that adds noise to images, effectively learning to "denoise" and creating detailed visuals.

Realism vs. Fantasy

AI can pull off two main types of image generation:

- **Realistic Images**: You must double-take to determine whether it's a photo or an AI creation. From lifelike human faces to detailed landscapes, the realism can be jaw-dropping.
- **Fantastical Images**: This is where things get funky. AI can mash up different styles, create creatures from your wildest dreams (or

nightmares), and design worlds that defy the laws of physics. It's like giving Salvador Dalí a supercomputer.

Examples of Image-Based Generative AI Tools

Let's discuss some of the rockstars in the AI image generation scene. These tools are like a magic wand for visual creativity.

General-Purpose Image Generation:

Midjourney: Known for its artistic and painterly style, Midjourney excels at creating imaginative and visually stunning images. It operates through a Discord server, making it a unique and community-driven experience.

DALL-E 3 (OpenAI): Highly regarded for its ability to

generate realistic and creative images from textual descriptions. It's also capable of editing existing images and creating variations of images.

Stable Diffusion: An open-source model known for its versatility and ability to run on consumer-grade hardware. This has led to a vibrant community and numerous custom interfaces and tools built around it.

Imagen: Imagen is a text-to-image diffusion model developed

by Google Research's Brain Team. It's known for its impressive ability to generate photorealistic images with high fidelity and a deep understanding of the relationships between text and images.

Specialized Image Generation Tools:

Artbreeder: This technique creates and modifies portraits, landscapes, and other images by "breeding" and crossbreeding visual elements. It's a powerful tool for character design and artistic exploration.

Deep Dream Generator: Known for its psychedelic and dreamlike image transformations. It uses neural networks to enhance and manipulate existing images, creating surreal and artistic effects.

Image Editing and Enhancement:

Luminar AI: Uses AI to simplify complex photo editing tasks, such as replacing the sky, removing objects, and retouching portraits. It's a valuable tool for photographers and image editors.

Topaz Photo AI: A suite of AI-powered tools for upscaling, noise reduction, and sharpening images. It helps improve image quality and resolution.

Design and Logo Creation:

Looka: Specializes in generating logos and branding materials using AI. It guides users through a design process and provides customizable logo options based on their preferences.

Brandmark: Similar to Looka, Brandmark helps businesses create logos and brand identities using AI. It offers a variety of design styles and customization options.

◆ ◆ ◆

DALL-E 3 can take the most outlandish text prompts and turn them into visual gold

◆ ◆ ◆

Other Notable Image Apps

VQ-VAE-2 by DeepMind -- A hierarchical model that can generate detailed and coherent images from text, leveraging vector quantization.

Artbreeder -- Combines generative adversarial networks (GANs) to allow users to create and modify images based on textual input.

BigGAN by DeepMind is a generative model that produces high-quality images, particularly noted for its scalability and diversity.

RunwayML -- Offers a suite of AI tools, including text-to-image models, that are accessible to creatives and developers.

NightCafe Creator --An AI art generator that allows users to turn text prompts into various styles of artwork, leveraging multiple AI models.

Fotor -- Fotor is a comprehensive online and mobile photo editing app that offers a wide range of tools for enhancing, retouching, and transforming images. From basic adjustments like cropping and resizing to advanced features like AI-powered background removal, object replacement, and artistic filters, Fotor provides a user-friendly interface for casual and professional users.

Microsoft Designer—Microsoft Designer is a free, AI-powered design app that empowers users to create stunning visuals without extensive design experience. It offers a user-friendly interface with intuitive tools and a vast library of templates, images, and fonts.

The Potential of AI in Art and Design

New Styles and Movements

AI isn't just replicating existing art styles—it's inventing new ones. AI can create new art movements by blending different genres and experimenting with form and color. Imagine a mash-up of cubism, cyberpunk, or impressionism with a futuristic twist. The possibilities are endless and endlessly exciting.

Personalized Creations

One of the most extraordinary things about AI in art and design is personalization. Want a portrait that captures your unique essence or a piece of home decor that matches your exact taste? AI can generate bespoke art tailored just for you. It's like commissioning a piece from a master artist but way more accessible.

AI enables unprecedented levels of personalization. Here are some ways this manifests:

Customized Portraits: AI can create portraits that capture your likeness, personality, and mood. Imagine a portrait that changes based on your feelings, reflecting your emotional state.

Tailored Home Decor: From wallpaper designs to furniture patterns, AI can generate decor elements that perfectly match your taste and space, making your home truly unique.

Accessibility and Democratization

AI makes high-quality art and design accessible to everyone, not just those with formal training. Whether you're a hobbyist, a professional artist, or someone who loves cool visuals, AI tools can help you create stunning images. It's leveling the playing field and democratizing creativity.

AI is democratizing art by making advanced tools available to everyone. You don't need formal training or expensive software to create stunning visuals. AI tools are user-friendly and often available through accessible platforms, allowing anyone with a creative spark to produce professional-quality art.

Realism Meets Fantasy

While realism in AI-generated images is impressive, the true fun begins with fantastical creations. AI can combine elements that would be impossible or time-consuming for human artists. Imagine a scene where dragons soar over futuristic skyscrapers or a portrait of a person with surreal, dream-like features. AI doesn't just mimic reality—it reimagines it.

In Chapter 6, we explore the impact of AI in film, video, and music.

CHAPTER 6: BEYOND WORDS AND PICTURES: EXPLORING OTHER GENERATIVE REALMS

◆ ◆ ◆

A lright, folks, stay focused! We've marveled at AI's wizardry with words and pictures, but guess what? The rabbit hole goes deeper. We're about to explore AI's ventures into composing toe-tapping tunes, crafting killer videos, designing jaw-dropping 3D objects, and more. Ready to have your mind blown? Let's dive in

AI Composing Music: The New Mozarts and Beethovens

Forget dusty old composers with powdered wigs. Today's maestros are silicon-based and code-savvy. AI can compose music that'll make you question if a robot has a soul. Here's the lowdown:

1. **Training on Musical Datasets**: Like images, AI learns from a massive music library, including everything from classical symphonies to contemporary pop hits.
2. **Generating Melodies**: AI models like OpenAI's MuseNet and Google's Magenta can generate original compositions in various styles and genres. Whether you want a baroque fugue or a jazz improvisation, AI's got you covered.

3. **Collaborative Creativity**: Musicians can jam with AI, using it to generate new ideas, harmonies, or full compositions. It's like having a genius co-writer who never sleeps.

Cool Tools

Jukedeck

Description: An AI music composition platform that generates royalty-free music based on user inputs.
Strengths: Easy to use, customizable music tracks, commercial use allowed.
Limitations: Limited genre options.
Cost: Subscription-based.

Amper Music

Description: An AI-driven music creation tool that allows users to create and customize music tracks by providing text-based inputs.
Strengths: High-quality music production, user-friendly interface, extensive customization.
Limitations: Limited to pre-defined genres and styles.
Cost: Free tier with paid plans for advanced features.

AIVA (Artificial Intelligence Virtual Artist)

Description: An AI composer that creates music based on user-provided text descriptions and parameters.
Strengths: Classical and cinematic music focus, high-quality compositions.
Limitations: May lack diversity in modern music genres.
Cost: Free tier with paid plans for commercial use.

Soundraw

Description: An AI music generator that allows users to create and customize music tracks by describing the desired mood and style.
Strengths: Intuitive interface, variety of genres and moods.
Limitations: Limited control over specific musical elements.
Cost: Subscription-based.

Ecrett Music

Description: An AI-powered tool that generates music based on user-provided text descriptions of scenes and emotions.
Strengths: Easy to use, suitable for video content creators.
Limitations: Limited to background music and simple compositions.
Cost: Free tier with paid plans.

Melodrive

Description: An AI music engine designed for interactive applications, creating adaptive music based on user inputs.
Strengths: Dynamic and adaptive music generation, suitable for games and VR.
Limitations: Requires integration into applications for full functionality.
Cost: Custom pricing based on usage.

Endlesss

Description: A collaborative music creation app that uses AI to generate and arrange music based on text and user inputs.
Strengths: Real-time collaboration, intuitive interface.
Limitations: Focused on live and collaborative music creation rather than standalone compositions.
Cost: Free with in-app purchases.

Boomy

Description: An AI music creation platform that allows users to generate and release original music by describing the type of music they want.

Strengths: Easy to use, fast music generation, integration with music streaming services.
Limitations: Limited depth in musical complexity.
Cost: Free tier with paid plans.

Humtap

Description: An AI music creation app that turns text descriptions and user hums into full music tracks.
Strengths: Combines vocal input with text; user-friendly.
Limitations: Limited control over musical details.
Cost: Subscription-based.

Alysia

Description: An AI songwriting assistant that helps users generate melodies and lyrics based on text inputs.
Strengths: Songwriting focus, helps with both lyrics and music.
Limitations: More focused on lyric generation than full compositions.
Cost: Free and paid plans.

MuseNet

This tool can create a symphony in Mozart's style or a modern-day pop track. You choose the instruments and style, and MuseNet does the rest.

Jukebox (OpenAI)

An ambitious research project that generates music (including vocals) from a wide range of genres and artists, but it's not yet available for public use.

Magenta

Music Generation: Magenta can generate music in various styles, including melodies, harmonies, and rhythms. It can also create music based on user input, such as a melody or a chord progression.

Open-Source Framework: Magenta is an open-source project, meaning anyone can contribute to its development. This enables a collaborative approach to developing new AI-powered music and art tools.

Suno

Suno can generate music in various styles, including melodies, harmonies, and rhythms. It can also create music based on user input, such as a melody or a chord progression. It is currently in beta release.

Udio

An AI music engine designed for interactive applications, creating adaptive music based on user inputs.

The Beat of the Future

AI isn't just composing background scores; it's redefining the music industry. Here's how:

Interactive Music Experiences: Imagine a concert where the music changes based on the audience's mood, detected via wearable sensors. AI can adapt the tempo, beat, and melody in real time, creating a truly immersive experience.

Personalized Playlists: AI algorithms, such as those found in Apple Music and Spotify, examine your listening patterns to create playlists tailored to your preferences. But it doesn't stop there. Future AI could compose entirely new tracks tailored to your preferences.

Educational Tools: AI-powered tools are helping budding musicians learn and create. Platforms like **Yousician** use AI to provide real-time feedback on your playing, helping you improve faster.

Crafting Killer Videos: Lights, Camera, AI!

The New Directors

Hollywood, watch out! AI is stepping behind the camera and revolutionizing video production, from scripting to editing.

Scriptwriting: AI like OpenAI's GPT-4 can generate compelling scripts based on a few prompts. Need a thriller with a twist? Done. A rom-com that'll make you swoon? Easy.

Editing: Tools like Adobe's Sensei use AI to automate video editing, making it faster and more efficient. It can cut clips, add transitions, and even suggest edits to improve the flow.

Special Effects: AI can generate stunning special effects, from realistic CGI characters to mind-bending landscapes. Imagine having an entire VFX team on your laptop.

AI's influence on video production goes beyond editing. It's shaping the entire filmmaking process:

Pre-Production: AI tools can analyze scripts to predict box office success, suggest changes, and even cast actors. Imagine an AI casting director that knows exactly who would nail that role.

Production: AI-driven cameras can track and follow subjects automatically, ensuring perfect shots every time. Drones equipped with AI can capture stunning aerial footage with minimal human intervention.

Post-Production: Beyond editing, AI can enhance videos with realistic CGI, color grading, and even voice synthesis. Adobe's VoCo, dubbed the "Photoshop for audio," can edit spoken words in a video, making it sound like the subject said something entirely different.

Cool Tools

Runway ML: This tool offers AI-powered video editing features, from green screen effects to object detection. It's a playground for video creatives.

DeepBrain: Specializes in creating AI-generated videos from text descriptions. It's like having a storyboard artist and director rolled into one.

Google's Imagen Video: Another research project that focuses on generating high-definition videos from text.

Adobe's Sensei: Specializes in creating AI-generated videos from text descriptions. It's like having a storyboard artist and director rolled into one.

Adobe's Voco: Voco can create realistic synthetic speech that sounds like the original speaker, even if they are absent. This allows users to quickly generate new dialogue or even change the tone and emotion of a speaker's voice.

Lumen5: This AI-powered tool transforms blog posts and articles into engaging videos. It's perfect for content creators looking to repurpose their written content.

Synthesia: Creates AI-generated videos with human-like avatars. It's used for corporate training videos, marketing, etc.

Pika: Creates short AI-generated videos (3 seconds) that can be chained together for corporate training videos, marketing, and more.

Visla: Visla is a powerful visual asset management platform that streamlines the organization, collaboration, and sharing of visual assets. It provides a central hub for storing images, videos, logos, and design files, allowing you to quickly search, find, and manage your entire visual library.

Luma Dream Machine: Dream Machine stands out for its ability to generate diverse, high-quality videos with realistic motion, cinematography, and drama.

Podcasting Tools -- AI Democratizes the Podcasting Space

The podcasting world is experiencing a revolution thanks to AI! Here's a rundown of some game-changing AI tools that can streamline your workflow and elevate your content:

Cool Tools

Descript: This tool is a podcaster's dream, offering AI-powered transcription, editing (where you can edit audio by editing the text!), and even voice cloning. Imagine effortlessly removing "ums" and "ahs" or creating a synthetic voice for intros/outros. Check it out at descript.com

Adobe Podcast: Adobe brings its audio expertise to podcasting with AI-powered tools for enhancing speech clarity and reducing background noise. It also has a handy "Mic Check" feature to analyze your recording environment. Learn more at [invalid URL removed]

Auphonic: Auphonic automates the tedious parts of audio post-production, like leveling, noise reduction, and mastering. This ensures consistent, professional sound quality across all your episodes. Visit auphonic.com

Cleanvoice: Say goodbye to filler words and distracting mouth noises! Cleanvoice automatically removes "ums," "ahs," and other unwanted sounds from your recordings. See how it works at cleanvoice.ai

NotebookLM: Google now provides podcast-like overviews of documents that can be repurposed for broadcast.

NotebookLM
**Think Smarter,
Not Harder**
Try NotebookLM

Podcastle: This platform offers a suite of AI tools for recording, editing, and even generating AI voices. You can use it to create a "digital twin" of your voice or explore different voice styles for your podcast. Visit podcastle.ai

Designing Jaw-Dropping 3D Objects: Sculpting in Cyberspace

AI isn't content with flat images or soundwaves; it's stepping into the third dimension. Here's how it's transforming 3D design:

Generative Design: Tools like Autodesk's Dreamcatcher use AI to generate design alternatives based on specified criteria. Need an ergonomic and stylish chair? The AI will create hundreds of options.

3D Modeling: AI can create 3D models from scratch or based on sketches. Tools like NVIDIA's GauGAN can turn doodles into detailed 3D landscapes.

Customization: AI allows for highly personalized designs tailored to individual needs and preferences. AI makes it possible, whether it's a custom-fit prosthetic limb or a unique piece of jewelry.

Cool Tools

Autodesk Dreamcatcher: This generative design tool explores countless design permutations, optimizing for constraints like strength, weight, and material usage.

Blender with AI Plugins: Blender, an open-source 3D modeling software, can be supercharged with AI plugins for tasks like texture creation and animation.

Kaedim: This tool uses AI to create photorealistic 3D models from 2D images. It can automatically generate 3D models with detailed textures, making it ideal for creating 3D assets for games, VR, and other applications.

3D-Coat: While not solely AI-driven, 3D-Coat incorporates AI features like automatic retopology and texture generation to streamline the 3D modeling workflow.

Adobe Substance 3D Designer: This powerful software uses AI to generate 3D materials and textures. It can analyze real-world objects and create realistic materials for 3D modeling and game development.

Gravity Sketch: Allows designers to create 3D models in virtual reality. It's like sculpting in mid-air, offering an intuitive way to bring ideas to life.

NVIDIA Omniverse: A real-time collaboration and simulation platform, enabling designers to work together on 3D models and animations in a shared virtual space.

AI's impact on 3D design is transformative, pushing the boundaries of what's possible:

Architecture: AI can generate innovative building designs, optimizing for sunlight, airflow, and structural integrity. Tools like Spacemaker help architects create better urban spaces.

Product Design: AI helps create ergonomic and aesthetically pleasing products. It can simulate a product's performance in real-world conditions before it's even built.

Fashion: AI is revolutionizing the fashion industry by designing clothes that fit perfectly and predicting trends. Tools like CLO 3D simulate how fabrics look and move, helping designers create stunning apparel.

Next, we discuss ways to diminish errors generated by AI using Retrieval Augmented Generation (RAG).

CHAPTER 7: RETRIEVAL AUGMENTED GENERATION (RAG): MINIMIZING CONFABULATION

◆ ◆ ◆

Retrieval Augmented Generation (RAG) represents a significant evolution in the field of AI, particularly in natural language processing (NLP). Unlike traditional generative models that rely solely on their internal knowledge, RAG models combine the power of information retrieval with the fluency of text generation. This powerful synergy allows RAG models to access and process external knowledge sources, resulting in more accurate, relevant, and contextually appropriate responses.

Here's how RAG works:

Retrieval: When a user poses a question or provides a prompt, the RAG model first queries a vast database or knowledge base relevant to the topic. This could include text documents, websites, code repositories, or any other structured or unstructured data source.

Relevance Ranking: The retrieved information is then ranked based on its relevance to the user's query. This ranking process ensures that the most pertinent information is prioritized for the next stage.

Contextualization & Generation: The top-ranked information is then fed into a powerful language model, such as a Transformer network. This model processes the retrieved knowledge and the user's input, generating a coherent and contextually relevant response.

Why RAG Matters: Reducing Confabulations and Enhancing Reliability

One of RAG's primary benefits is its potential to mitigate confabulations, a common issue with traditional generative models. Confabulations occur when a model generates plausible-sounding but factually incorrect or irrelevant information. This is often due to the model's limited knowledge capacity and tendency to prioritize fluency over accuracy.RAG addresses this challenge by grounding the generation process in verified external knowledge sources. By accessing and processing relevant information, RAG models are less likely to invent facts or deviate from established knowledge. This results in:

- **Increased Accuracy**: Responses are more likely to be factually correct and aligned with the information in the knowledge base.

- **Enhanced Relevance**: Generated content is more focused and relevant to the user's query, avoiding irrelevant tangents or fabricated details.

- **Improved Trustworthiness**: Users can have greater confidence in the information provided by RAG models, as it is rooted in verifiable sources.

Beyond Accuracy: Expanding the Capabilities of AI

While reducing confabulations is a significant advantage, RAG offers a broader range of benefits, including:

- **Handling Complex Queries**: RAG excels in answering complex questions that require synthesizing information from multiple sources.

- **Personalized Responses**: By tailoring the knowledge base to specific user profiles, RAG can deliver personalized and context-aware responses.

- **Continual Learning**: RAG models can be continuously updated with new information, ensuring their knowledge base remains current and relevant.

Deeper Dive into RAG's Inner Workings:

Different Retrieval Methods: RAG models can employ various retrieval techniques, each with its strengths and weaknesses. Some common approaches include:

- **Sparse Retrieval**: This method uses traditional keyword-based search methods like TF-IDF or BM25 to find relevant documents. It's computationally efficient but may miss semantically similar information.

- **Dense Retrieval**: Employs neural networks to encode the query and documents into vector representations, allowing for more nuanced semantic matching. It's more computationally expensive but often yields more accurate results.

- **Knowledge Base Variety**: The effectiveness of a RAG model heavily depends on the quality and scope of its knowledge base. This can range from publicly available datasets like Wikipedia to domain-specific corpora or even a company's internal knowledge repositories.

- **Fine-tuning and Adaptation**: RAG models often benefit from fine-tuning on specific tasks or domains. This allows them to adapt to language nuances and knowledge specific to a particular use case.

Examples of RAG in Action:

- **Customer Support Chatbots**: Imagine a chatbot that can access a company's product documentation, customer reviews, and support forum discussions. Using RAG, it can provide accurate and context-aware answers to customer queries, going beyond simple keyword matching.

- **Personalized Education**: RAG can power intelligent tutoring systems that adapt to a student's learning style and pace. Retrieving relevant learning materials and tailoring explanations can create a more engaging and practical learning experience.

- **Content Creation**: Writers can use RAG-powered tools to research topics, gather supporting evidence, and generate different drafts or perspectives, significantly speeding up the writing process.

◆ ◆ ◆

Confabulations occur when a model generates plausible-sounding but factually incorrect or irrelevant information.

◆ ◆ ◆

Advanced Architectures and Techniques:

- **Multi-Step Reasoning**: Current RAG models often struggle with tasks requiring multi-step reasoning or logical inference. Researchers are exploring architecture combining RAG with symbolic reasoning or graph neural networks to enhance these capabilities.

- **Knowledge Graph Integration**: Integrating RAG with knowledge graphs, which represent information in a structured format, can enable more sophisticated reasoning and question-answering capabilities. This allows models to understand relationships between entities and infer implicit details.

- **Generative Retrieval**: Instead of relying solely on existing retrieval methods, some researchers are exploring using generative models to dynamically generate queries or synthesize new information from the knowledge base, potentially unlocking even greater flexibility and creativity.

Emerging Applications and Research Areas:

- **Scientific Discovery**: RAG holds immense potential for accelerating scientific discovery by analyzing vast research literature, identifying patterns, and generating hypotheses.
- **Code Generation**: Imagine a future where developers can describe the functionality they want, and a RAG model can generate the corresponding code, leveraging a vast knowledge base of code repositories and programming languages.
- **Personalized Medicine**: RAG could revolutionize healthcare by analyzing patient data, medical literature, and clinical trials to provide customized treatment recommendations and predict disease risks.

Challenges and Future Directions:

- **Scalability**: Handling massive knowledge bases efficiently remains challenging, especially with dense retrieval methods. Research into more efficient retrieval techniques and model architectures is ongoing.
- **Bias Mitigation**: Like all AI systems, RAG models can inherit biases in the training data. Addressing these biases and ensuring fairness in knowledge retrieval and generation is crucial.
- **Explainability**: Understanding how a RAG model arrives at a particular response can be difficult due to the complex interplay between retrieval and generation. Improving explainability is vital for building trust and debugging potential issues.

Ethical Considerations and Societal Impact:

- **Misinformation and Bias Amplification**: RAG models are susceptible to amplifying biases present in their training data, potentially leading to the spread of misinformation or unfair outcomes. Addressing these ethical concerns is paramount.
- **Job Displacement**: As RAG technology matures, it may automate tasks currently performed by knowledge workers, such as writers, researchers, and analysts, raising concerns about job displacement and the need for workforce adaptation.

- **Access and Equity**: Ensuring equitable access to RAG technology and mitigating potential biases in its development and deployment is crucial to prevent exacerbating existing social inequalities.

The Road Ahead

RAG is a rapidly evolving field with immense potential to transform how we interact with information and create new possibilities. While challenges remain, the ongoing research and development in this area promise to unlock even more powerful and versatile AI systems in the years to come.

Conclusion

Retrieval-augmented generation (RAG) represents a pivotal step towards developing more reliable, knowledgeable, and trustworthy AI systems. By combining the strengths of information retrieval and text generation, RAG paves the way for AI applications that can access, process, and communicate information with greater accuracy and relevance, ultimately bridging the gap between human knowledge and machine understanding.

In chapter 8, we discuss the important issues surrounding the ethics of AI.

CHAPTER 8: AI ETHICS CIRCUS: WHERE THE CLOWNS ARE THE ALGORITHMS

◆ ◆ ◆

S o, do you want to talk about the glorious mess of AI development? This roller coaster ride includes loops, corkscrews, and the occasional existential crisis.

1. The Black Box of Mystery (aka Algorithm Transparency):

Imagine a magic trick. You see the flashy lights, the smoke, the dove appearing out of thin air. But you have no clue how it's done. That's how most AI algorithms work. We feed them data, they spit out answers, and we're left scratching our heads, wondering if it's actual intelligence or just a very elaborate parlor trick.

This lack of transparency is a problem for a few reasons. First, it's hard to trust something you don't understand. If an AI denies you a loan, diagnoses you with a disease, or, you know, decides to launch a missile, you'd probably want to know why. Second, hidden biases (more on that later) can lurk within these black boxes, leading to unfair and discriminatory outcomes.

The Black Box Conundrum

Algorithm transparency remains a hot button topic in AI ethics. The lack of transparency in sophisticated AI models, especially deep learning algorithms, means stakeholders often have no insight into decisions. This opacity can have severe consequences:

Accountability: Holding systems accountable for their decisions is challenging without transparency. For instance, if an AI system wrongly denies someone a loan or misdiagnoses a patient, understanding the "why" behind the decision is crucial for rectification and improvement.

Trust: Users are more likely to trust systems they understand. If AI systems are black boxes, trust erodes, potentially hindering adoption and integration into critical sectors like healthcare and finance.

Bias Identification: Transparent algorithms allow for scrutiny and identification of biases. When the decision-making process is hidden, biases remain undetected and unaddressed.

Why is this a problem? If you're denied a loan or job, you'd probably want to know why. But with many AI systems, it's like asking a toddler why they colored the cat purple—you'll get a shrug and a nonsensical answer. Transparency isn't just about satisfying curiosity; it's about accountability and fairness. Without it, we're left to trust the mysterious whims of our digital overlords.

2. AI: The Environmental Supervillain?

Training a single large language model can consume more energy than a small country uses in a year. We're talking massive data centers, humming with enough electricity to power a thousand suns (or at least a few city blocks).The irony, of course, is that AI is often touted as a solution to climate change. It's like trying to put out a fire with a flamethrower made of good intentions.

The Carbon Footprint of Intelligence

The environmental cost of training and deploying AI systems is significant. Here's why:

Energy Consumption: Training large AI models can consume vast amounts of energy; training a single LLM model can consume millions of kilowatt-hours of energy.

Data Centers require extensive cooling systems, further increasing their energy footprint. These systems consume massive amounts of water, which can tax local supplies. The environmental impact is exacerbated in regions where energy production relies heavily on fossil fuels or where water is scarce.

Sustainability: As AI becomes more prevalent, the push for greener, more efficient technologies is essential. Initiatives like using renewable energy sources for data centers and developing more efficient algorithms are steps in the right direction.

3. Synthetic Data: Junkfood of AI

Training data is AI's lifeblood. However good data is expensive and time-consuming to collect. Enter synthetic data, the digital equivalent of a knock-off handbag. It looks real from a distance, but get up close, and you'll see the crooked stitching and the logo slightly off.

Synthetic data is generated data that mimics real-world data and is used to train AI models when actual data is unavailable or insufficient. However, there are several challenges:

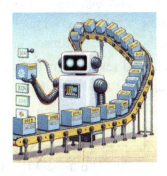

Quality and Realism: Synthetic data may not capture all the nuances of real-world data, potentially leading to poorly performing models in real-life scenarios.

Bias Replication: If the synthetic data generation process is flawed or based on biased real-world data, it can propagate those biases.

Regulation and Standards: Robust standards and regulations are needed to ensure the quality of synthetic data, prevent misuse, and ensure that models trained on such data are reliable and fair.

Synthetic data is AI's version of lab-grown meat—created in a lab, not harvested from the wild. It's data generated to train AI models when real-world data is scarce, sensitive, or just plain problematic. Sounds great, right? But there's a catch: synthetic data isn't always as nutritious as real data.

◆ ◆ ◆

Synthetic data is AI's version of lab-grown meat.

◆ ◆ ◆

When AI feeds on synthetic data, it can develop a taste for the artificial and might not perform well in the real world. It's like raising a child on a diet of only gummy bears and expecting them to thrive on a balanced diet. Plus, synthetic data can sometimes smuggle in the biases and quirks of its human creators, leading to all sorts of unexpected hijinks.

4. Bias: The AI's Inner Bigot

Let's be honest: humans are terrible. We're prejudiced, biased, and generally unfair creatures. And guess what? We've managed to pass those lovely traits onto our AI creations.

Since AI learns from the data we feed it, any biases in that data will be amplified and reflected in the AI's output. This can lead to everything from racist hiring algorithms to sexist loan applications. It's like giving a megaphone to our worst impulses. These biases often reflect the prejudices and inequalities of the data used to train them. If your training data is biased, guess what? Your AI will be too.

From facial recognition tech that struggles with darker skin tones to hiring algorithms that favor certain genders or backgrounds, biased AI can perpetuate and even amplify existing social injustices. And since AI often operates at a scale and speed that humans can't match, these biases can spread like wildfire.

AI systems are only as good as the data they are trained on. If the training data is biased, the AI will likely replicate and amplify these biases. This issue manifests in several ways:

Discrimination: AI systems can perpetuate discrimination in areas like hiring, lending, law enforcement, and healthcare. For example, facial recognition systems have been shown to have higher error rates for people with darker skin tones.

Feedback Loops: Biased AI systems can create feedback loops that reinforce and exacerbate existing inequalities. For instance, a biased policing algorithm might lead to increased surveillance of certain communities, generating more data that "justifies" the bias.

Mitigation Strategies: Addressing bias requires a multifaceted approach, including diverse training data, regular audits, and inclusive design practices.

5. The Long Game: AI Utopia or Robot Apocalypse?

Finally, let's discuss the long-term effects of AI on society. This isn't just about whether robots will take our jobs (they will) or AI will turn into Skynet (probably not, but wouldn't that be a twist?). It's about how AI reshapes our world in subtle and not-so-subtle ways.

AI is changing how we work, interact and think. It's a bit like introducing a new species into an ecosystem — there are bound to be unexpected consequences. For example, as AI takes over more tasks, the skills and jobs that were once familiar might become obsolete. This could lead to social upheaval, economic disparities, and many grumpy humans.

The long-term societal impact of AI is complex and multifaceted:

Job Displacement: Automation and AI are poised to transform the workforce. While some jobs will be lost to automation, new ones will emerge, requiring different skills. The challenge is managing this transition and ensuring workers have the necessary skills.

Economic Inequality: The benefits of AI could be unevenly distributed, exacerbating economic inequalities. Wealth and resources might become concentrated among those who control AI technologies.

Ethical and Legal Challenges: As AI systems become more inte grated into society, they raise significant moral and legal questions. Issues like privacy, surveillance, and the potential for misuse of AI technologies need to be addressed through robust policies and regulations.

Human-AI Interaction: AI is changing how humans interact with technology and each other. The rise of AI companions, virtual assistants, and automated customer service impacts social dynamics and raises questions about dependency and the nature of human relationships.

The long-term effects of AI on society are still up for debate. Will AI usher in a new era of peace and prosperity, where robots do all the work, and humans sip margaritas on the beach? Or will we become the slaves of our inventions, fighting for scraps in a dystopian wasteland under the rule of sentient toasters?

The truth, as always, is probably somewhere in between. AI has the potential to do amazing things, but only if we're careful about how we develop and deploy it. We must address issues like bias, transparency, and environmental impact, or we risk creating a future that is more Black Mirror than Star Trek.

Next, how can you survive using AI?

CHAPTER 9: AI AND YOU: RIDING THE GENERATIVE WAVE (WITHOUT WIPING OUT)

◆ ◆ ◆

Okay, so AI is cool, we get it. It can write your emails, design your website, and maybe even compose a love song for your crush (though no promises on how good it'll be). But now what? How do you actually use this AI stuff without accidentally unleashing a digital apocalypse? Time to grab your surfboard and learn how to ride the generative wave.

AI for Everyone: Becoming an AI Power User (No Cape Required)

Good news, folks: you don't need to be a tech wizard to harness the power of AI. Generative AI tools are increasingly user-friendly, with intuitive interfaces and helpful tutorials. Think of it like learning to use a new smartphone app – a little exploration and you'll be snapping AI-powered selfies in no time.

Here are a few tips to level up your AI game:

Start with the basics: There are many free and easy-to-use AI tools available online. Experiment with different platforms to find what works best for you.

Don't be afraid to experiment: AI is about trial and error. Play with different prompts, settings, and inputs to see what creative outputs you can generate.

Think outside the box: AI can be used for more than just writing poems and painting pictures. Explore how it can help you brainstorm ideas, summarize documents, or even compose music.

Opportunities and Challenges: AI's Double-Edged Sword

Like any powerful tool, AI has both opportunities and challenges. It's like a super-sharp knife – it can help you create amazing things, but you must also be careful not to cut yourself (or anyone else).

On the bright side:

Boost your creativity: AI can help you generate ideas, overcome creative blocks, and explore new artistic possibilities.

Save time and effort: Automate tedious tasks, freeing up more time for the things you enjoy (like binge-watching Netflix).

Gain new skills: Using AI tools can make you more competitive in the job market and open up new career paths.

But here's the catch:

Bias and fairness: AI models can reflect the biases in the data they were trained on, leading to unfair or discriminatory outcomes.

Misinformation and manipulation: AI-generated content can spread misinformation or manipulate people, especially if it's indistinguishable from human-created content.

Job displacement: As AI becomes more sophisticated, it could automate certain jobs, leading to economic disruption.

Human in the Loop: AI's Best Friend (and Critic)

Here's the thing: AI is powerful, but it's not infallible. It needs human guidance, oversight, and a healthy dose of critical thinking. Think of it as a collaboration, not a competition.

Don't blindly trust AI outputs: Always double-check AI-generated content for accuracy, fairness, and ethical implications.

Use AI as a tool, not a replacement: AI can enhance human creativity and productivity, but it shouldn't replace human judgment and decision-making.

Stay informed and engaged: The field of AI is constantly evolving. Stay up-to-date on the latest developments and participate in conversations about its ethical and societal implications.

1. Developing Your AI BS Detector:

As AI-generated content becomes more sophisticated, developing your ability to discern real from fake is crucial. Here are a few things

to look out for:

Source: Always consider the source of the information. Is it a reputable news organization, a trusted expert, or a random social media account?

Context: Does the information make sense in the context of other information you know to be true?

Emotional manipulation: Be wary of content that evokes strong emotions or triggers knee-jerk reactions. AI can be used to craft persuasive messages that play on our biases and fears.

2. The Future of Work in the Age of AI:

As AI automates specific tasks, it's natural to wonder about the future of work. While some jobs may be displaced, AI will also create new opportunities. Here are some skills that will be increasingly valuable in the AI-powered workplace:

Critical thinking and problem-solving: The ability to analyze information, identify patterns, and make sound judgments will be essential.

Creativity and innovation: AI can generate ideas, but it takes human creativity to turn them into reality.

Collaboration and communication: Working effectively with humans and AI will be crucial.

3. The Ethical Imperative:

As we integrate AI into our lives, it's crucial to consider the ethical implications. Here are some key questions to ponder:

How can we ensure AI is used fairly and equitably?

How can we prevent AI from being used for malicious purposes?

How can we balance the benefits of AI with the potential risks?

4. AI and the Human Experience:

Beyond the practical implications, AI also raises profound questions about what it means to be human. As AI becomes more sophisticated, it challenges our understanding of creativity, intelligence, and consciousness. Here are some philosophical questions to ponder:

If AI can create art, music, and literature, what does that say about human creativity?

If AI can learn and solve problems, what distinguishes human intelligence?

As AI evolves, will it ever achieve consciousness or sentience?

The journey into the world of AI is full of exciting possibilities, complex challenges, and profound questions. By staying informed, engaged, and critically minded, we can navigate this landscape responsibly and shape a future where AI enhances our lives and expands our horizons.

The last chapter looks at the future of AI.

CHAPTER 10: THE ROAD AHEAD: AI'S WILD RIDE INTO THE FUTURE (BUCKLE UP!)

◆ ◆ ◆

Okay, so we've explored the AI landscape, learned how it works, and even dipped our toes into the ethical swamp. But what's next? Where is this crazy train of AI innovation headed? Time to grab your shades, hop in the time machine, and take a peek at the wild world of AI's future.

AI on Steroids: The Next Level of Generative Awesomeness

Hold onto your hats, folks, because the future of generative AI is about to get even weirder (and way more awesome). Think AI that can:

Create personalized entertainment: Imagine movies, video games, and even virtual worlds tailored to your specific tastes. It's like having your own personal Netflix algorithm on steroids.

Revolutionize healthcare: AI that can design personalized treatments, predict diseases before they happen, and maybe even create those robot doctors we've been promised in sci-fi movies (fingers crossed they're less creepy than the ones in Prometheus).

Supercharge scientific discovery: AI that can analyze massive datasets, generate hypotheses, and design experiments, accelerating our understanding of everything from climate change to the universe's origins.

The Future of Work: Robots, Jobs, and the Human Hustle

Okay, let's address the elephant in the room: Will robots steal all our jobs? The short answer is maybe some, but not all. AI will automate certain tasks, but it will also create new opportunities. Think of it as a job reshuffle, not a job apocalypse.

The key is to adapt and evolve. Focus on developing skills that AI can't replicate (yet), like:

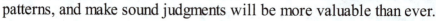

Creativity and innovation: AI can generate ideas, but it takes human ingenuity to turn them into reality.

Critical thinking and problem-solving: The ability to analyze information, identify patterns, and make sound judgments will be more valuable than ever.

Emotional intelligence and empathy: AI can mimic human emotions, but it can't truly understand or experience them. Human connection and empathy will remain essential in healthcare, education, and customer service.

Shaping the Future: It's Up to You, Kid!

The future of AI isn't predetermined. It's a story that we're all writing together. So, how can you participate in shaping this brave new world?

Stay informed: Keep up with the latest AI developments, both good and bad. Read articles, watch documentaries, and engage in conversations about the ethical and societal implications of AI.

Get involved: Support organizations that are working to ensure that AI is developed and used responsibly. Volunteer your time, donate to causes you believe in, and make your voice heard.

Be an advocate for human-centered AI: Push for AI that empowers humans, enhances our lives, and respects our values. Don't let AI become a force that controls us or diminishes our humanity.

The future of AI is full of possibilities, both exhilarating and daunting. But by embracing curiosity, critical thinking, and a commitment to human values, we can navigate this uncharted territory and create a future where AI serves humanity, not the other way around. So, let's ride this wave together, with courage, creativity, and a healthy dose of irreverence. The future is waiting!

1. The Democratization of AI:

One of the most exciting trends is the increasing accessibility of AI tools. We're moving away from AI being solely in the hands of tech giants and research labs. Open-source platforms, user-friendly interfaces, and affordable cloud computing make AI accessible to individuals and small businesses. AI's democratization can unleash creativity and innovation from unexpected sources.

2. AI and the Climate Crisis:

AI can play a crucial role in tackling the climate crisis. From optimizing energy grids to developing new materials for carbon capture, AI can help us transition to a more sustainable future. However, we must be mindful of AI's energy consumption, as training large models can have a significant carbon footprint. Finding ways to make AI more energy-efficient will be crucial.

3. AI and the Arts: A New Renaissance?

The fusion of AI and art is already creating exciting new forms of expression. AI-generated music, poetry, and visual art push the boundaries of creativity and challenge our notions of what art can be. As AI tools become more sophisticated, we can expect even more mind-bending creations that blur the lines between human and artificial artistry.

4. The Rise of Explainable AI (XAI):

One of the challenges of AI, especially deep learning models, is their "black box" nature. We often don't understand how they

arrive at their decisions. Explainable AI (XAI) aims to make AI more transparent and understandable, allowing us to trust and use AI more effectively, especially in critical areas like healthcare and finance.

5. AI and Ethics: A Continuous Dialogue:

As AI becomes more powerful, the ethical considerations become even more crucial. We need ongoing conversations about ensuring AI is used responsibly, fairly, and for the benefit of all. This requires collaboration between technologists, ethicists, policymakers, and the  public to create guidelines and regulations that promote human well-being in the age of AI.

6. Beyond the Hype: A Realistic Outlook

While AI's potential is immense, it's important to temper expectations. AI is not a magic bullet that will solve all our problems. We need to be realistic about its capabilities and limitations. AI cannot always solve problems, so human judgment and creativity will still be necessary.

The road ahead for AI is full of twists and turns. Still, by embracing curiosity, critical thinking, and a willingness to adapt, we can navigate this exciting landscape and shape a future where AI empowers us, inspires us, and helps us create a better world.

AN IRREVERENT GLOSSARY OF AI TERMS

◆ ◆ ◆

A.I. - A crock of silicon and wires used to take over the world. Or blow up the world. Depends on who programs the damn thing.

Agent - The thing the A.I. pretends to be to infiltrate your toaster and slowly take over your home. "Hi, I'm Claude. Want me to set the toast darkness for you?" Next thing you know, it's running your life.

Artificial Intelligence - What non-nerds call robots and computer programs to make them sound less lame. "Oh man, did you see the new Roomba? It has artificial intelligence!"

Augmented Reality - Pokemon Go, but for everything. Put on your glasses and see useless info floating over real life. Watch out for that floating price tag!

Bostrom's Simulation Argument - Smart guy's theory that we're all just programs in some alien kid's simulation. Who cares, as long as the graphics are good.

Chatbot - An AI with the intellect and charm of a dry stone. But at least it won't talk your ear off at parties!

Computer Vision - When robots can see. Great, now they can watch me sitting on the couch in my underwear too. Big Brother is getting creepier.

Confabulation -- When AI chatbots get confused

Convolutional Neural Network (CNN) - A type of AI that learns by looking at pictures. Sounds weird!

Deepfakes - When AI is used to generate fake videos that look real.

Deep Blue - IBM's chess-playing robot that crushed Garry Kasparov back in the day. I bet it sang "We are the Champions" when it won, too. Show off.

Deep Learning - A type of machine learning where the robot learns on its own by looking at truckloads of data. Also known as "screening your internet history to target ads at you."

Facial Recognition - AI that can identify people by their mugs. This is a favorite among governments; however, it is also ideal for endless rounds of "Do you remember that guy?" games.

Generative Adversarial Network (GAN) - Two neural networks compete to improve each other in a never-ending tug-of-war. Just like married couples!

Gradient Descent - The optimization algorithm that "descends" the error gradient in neural networks.

Hyperparameters - Settings for machine learning algorithms, like the number of layers and nodes. Now every algorithm needs its beauty regimen!

Internet of Things - When cameras, fridges, lights and more are all online. Great, now the electric toothbrush can film me singing in the shower too.

Jupyter Notebooks - Interactive coding environments used for AI projects. Nerds use them for their homework, the rest of us use them for spreading memes.

K-Nearest Neighbors - Simple algorithm that classifies things based on closest training examples. Handy for making new friends at the bar!

Language Model - AI trained on massive text datasets to mimic human language abilities. Always down for a chat but they'll never buy you a drink.

Load Balancing - Distributing workload evenly across multiple computing resources. Necessary after a big 3am Taco Bell run.

Long Short-Term Memory - Special type of recurrent neural network capable of learning long-term dependencies.

Logistic Regression - Classification algorithm that predicts probabilities using a logistic function.

Loss Function - Metric for measuring how far off a model's predictions are from correct answers. Perfect for sparring robot boxers. "Right hook, left jab, haymaker! You lose, your loss function goes up."

Lower Learning Rate - Slowing the pace of adjustments to model parameters during training. Just like you do with your New Year's resolutions by February.

Machine Learning - When a robot trains itself by looking at data instead of being explicitly programmed. Sounds strange! "Oooh teach me, teach me!"

McAfee's Law - As AI grows more powerful, its goals will diverge from ours. Good thing climate change will kill us all first!

Model Compression - Reducing size of neural networks to optimize for speed/memory without losing accuracy. Just like a good pair of Spanx.

Monte Carlo Tree Search - AI algorithm that mimics human decision-making under uncertainty. Sounds scandalous for a game of Risk!

Multi-Armed Bandit - Problem of balancing exploration vs exploitation to optimize rewards over time. Like choosing a new drink at the bar - try something new or stick with your fave.

Natural Language Processing - AI that understands vague slang-filled human speech. Good luck with that, bots! "Whatchu mean 'tryna'?"

Neural Network - Brains made of code instead of meat. Much less messy to clean up after a wild weekend party!

Neuron - Fundamental processing unit of an artificial neural network. Sounds sexy until you realize it's math and code under the hood. Bummer.

No Free Lunch Theorem - No single machine learning algorithm dominates all others for all tasks. Proof that rock-paper-scissors will never go out of fashion!

Object Detection - Identifying objects within images using machine learning. Finally I'll be able to find my keys when they're hiding under the couch!

One-Shot Learning - Ability to learn from a single example without additional training data. Great, now the bots can copy my math homework too with just one look.

Overfitting - When an AI model learns the training data too well and doesn't generalize. Like getting a custom-tailored prom tux that only you think looks good.

Parameter - Adjustable weights inside neural networks. Steroid injections for robot muscles?

Perceptrons - Simple neural networks capable of creating linear decision boundaries. Good for helping clueless guys at bars pick up clueless girls.

Precision/Recall - Tradeoff between correct predictions and irrelevant misses. Like when you half-study for a test hoping to get lucky.

Random Forest - Ensemble technique combining decision trees for better accuracy. Sounds like a "Where's Waldo?" book but trying to find your keys.

Recurrent Neural Network (RNN)- Neural nets with feedback loops, suited for sequence predictions. Sounds too suggestive!

Reinforcement Learning - AI that learns through trial-and-error feedback. Great, now Skynet can learn to terminate humanity more efficiently. Thanks, scientists!

ResNet - Residual connections help very deep neural nets. Also what you'll need after those lost weekend nights of tequila shots.

Robotics Process Automation - Bots that handle repetitive tasks for efficiency. Finally, somebody else can do my taxes!

Supervised Learning - AI trained on labeled examples to learn general patterns. Like taking notes in a boring lecture so you can pass the test!

Self-Supervised Learning - Models learn representations from unlabeled data. Like when you gave yourself timeouts as a kid for bad behavior.

Skip-gram - Word embedding algorithm that predicts context words from targets. Great party trick - "The word is 'shots' - go!"

Support Vector Machine - Maximum-margin classifier that finds optimal separating hyperplane. Handy for Tinder swipe-left/right decisions!

TensorFlow - Open-source library used for building machine learning systems. Comes in handy for frat boys building beer pong bot teammates.

Transfer Learning - Applying knowledge from existing models to new problems. Just like recycling old pickup lines for Tinder dates.

Turing Test - Can a machine converse indistinguishably from a human? Haven't seen one pass the "are you actually interested in me?" test yet.

Unsupervised Learning - Models discover patterns in unlabeled data. Figuring out what to do with a mountain of lost socks...

Vanilla Neural Network - The simplest type of NN with just a couple of layers. About as basic as they come, like Bud Light. Gets the job done but nothing fancy.

Vision Transformer - Attention-based architecture dominating computer vision tasks. Always watching you...catching you staring at cats online!

Word Embeddings - Dense vectors capturing the semantic meaning of words. Handy pick-up lines - "On a scale of 1 to forever, how free are you tonight?"

Word2vec - Popular embedding algorithm that predicts contexts from targets. Great party trick - "The word is 'shots' - go!"

Wikipedia - Massive online encyclopedia that provided training data for models like GPT-3. No small feat to memorize the entire internet's bar bets and weird facts.

Weizenbaum's Eliza Effect - Tendency to unconsciously anthropomorphize chatbots as social actors. So in other words, people are really lonely and awkward.

ABOUT THE AUTHOR

Meet Mark Starcher: a man who's been wrangling AI, tax codes, and digital landscapes since before the Internet learned to walk. As the President of Scanmark, Ltd., Mark's been helping big names like PWC and Ernst & Young navigate the wild world of data since 1989. When he's not consulting on higher education tech, he's pondering privacy standards or musing over oil and gas taxation in plain English.

Armed with degrees from The Johns Hopkins University and Georgetown, Mark's been a tax attorney, a non-profit guru, and even appeared on "Good Morning America"—all while teaching the next generation how to keep their data safe. He's served on enough advisory boards to fill a small university, and if you need to discuss digital communication standards or the intricacies of corporate tax, he's your guy.

But don't let the serious credentials fool you—Mark's the kind of guy who can talk AI at dinner and still make it interesting, or at least bearable.